STEP INTO...
THE ROMAN EMPIRE

Philip Steele

Consultant: Jenny Hall, Museum of London

LORENZ BOOKS
LONDON • NEW YORK • SYDNEY • BATH

This edition first published by Lorenz Books in 1997

©1997 Anness Publishing Limited

Lorenz Books is an imprint of Anness Publishing Limited, Hermes House, 88-89 Blackfriars Road London SE1 8HA

This edition distributed in Canada by Raincoast Books, 8680 Cambie Street, Vancouver, British Columbia, V6P 6M9

ISBN 1 85967 526 3

A CIP Catalogue record for this book is available from the British Library

Publisher: Joanna Lorenz
Managing Editor: Sue Grabham
Senior Editor: Ambreen Husain
Designer: John Jamieson
Illustration: Stuart Carter
Photography: John Freeman
Stylist: Thomasina Smith

Anness Publishing would like to thank the following children for modelling for this book: Mohammed Asfar, Leon R. Banton, Afsana Begum, Ha Chu, Paula Dent, Frankie Timothy Junior Elliot, Rikky Charles Healey, Eva Rivera/Razbadavskite, Simon Thexton, Shereen Thomas and Ha Vinh.

PICTURE CREDITS

b=bottom, t=top, c=centre, l=left, r=right

Lesley and Roy Adkins Picture Library: pages 5cr, 13t, 31bl, 35b, 38l, 39b and 55tl; Ancient Art and Arichitecture Collection Ltd: pages 8b, 8l, 9tl, 9tc, 11tl, 14b, 21tr, 21cl, 21cr, 24/25, 27r, 31bl, 32b, 33tr, 33br, 36, 41t, 42b, 49tr, 50bl, 52tr, 52bl, 54tr, 57tl, 61bl and front cover; A-Z Botanical Collection Ltd: page 53br; The Bridgeman Art Library: page 13b; The British Museum: pages 22r, 23tr, 23cr, 23bl, 28c, 28r, 30l, 42c, 48bl, 48br, 49b, 52br, 57b and 63bc; Peter Clayton: pages 18l, 25cr, 34tl and 37bc; C M Dixon: pages 10l, 12bl, 14t, 15bl, 17tl, 17cr, 20bl, 24bl, 25tr, 25br, 26l, 26r, 27l, 29tl, 29tc, 29tr, 30r, 32-33, 33bl, 34tr, 34b, 35t, 35c, 37tl, 37tr, 38br, 40cl, 40tr, 41bl, 44t, 45tl, 45cl, 45bl, 47t, 47c, 48tr, 49tl, 50tl, 50br, 51tl, 55tr, 55b, 56l, 57tr, 58tr, 58bl, 58br, 60l, 60r, 62t, 63c, title page, front cover and back cover; Geoscience Features Picture Library: page 61tr; Sonia Halliday Photographs: pages 15tl, 38tr and 63l; Michael Holford Photographs: pages 3t, 5tr, 12tr, 12br, 16, 22l, 28l, 29br, 37bl, 40bl, 40br, 45br, 46bl, 51tr, 51bl, 53bl, 54bl, 61tl and 62br; Simon James: pages 43tr and 43br; Mary Evans Picture Library: pages 9bl, 9br, 10r, 20tr, 29bl, 44b, 54br, 56r, and 59t; Planet Earth Pictures Ltd: page 5b; Tony Stone Images: pages 4-5; Visual Arts Library: pages 39tr and 46-47; Werner Forman Archive: pages 21bl and 53t; Zefa: pages 8r, 15br and 47b.

Printed and bound in Hong Kong

10 9 8 7 6 5 4 3 2 1

CONTENTS

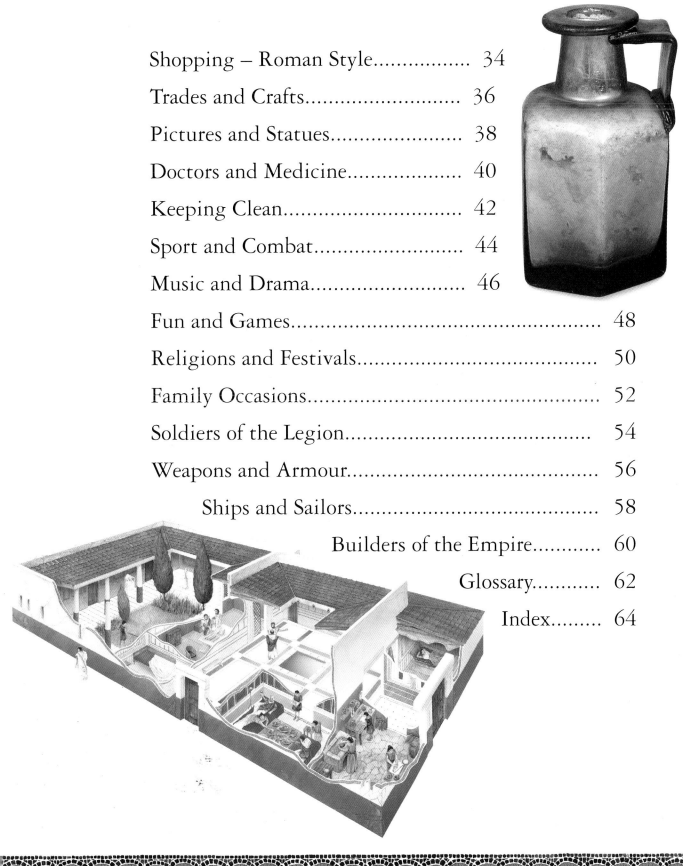

The Story of Rome

THE CITY OF ROME today is a bustling place, full of traffic and crowds. But if you could travel back in time to around 800BC, you would find only a few small villages on peaceful, wooded hillsides along the banks of the river Tiber. According to legend, Rome was founded here in 753BC. In the centuries that followed, the Romans came to dominate Italy and the Mediterranean. They farmed and traded and fought for new lands. Rome grew to become the centre of a vast empire that stretched across Europe into Africa and Asia. The Empire lasted for centuries and brought a sophisticated way of life to vast numbers of people. Many Roman buildings and artefacts still survive to show us what life was like in the Roman Empire.

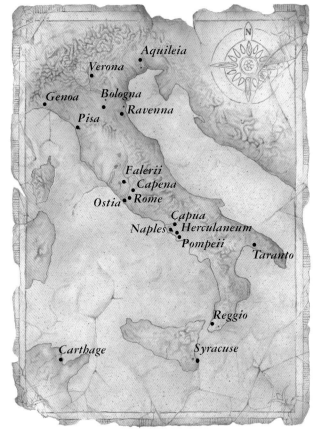

ROMAN ITALY
As the city of Rome prospered, the Romans gradually conquered neighbouring tribes. By 250BC they controlled most of Italy. This map shows some of the important towns and cities of that time.

ANCIENT AND MODERN
In Rome today, people live alongside the temples, marketplaces and public buildings of the past. This is the Colosseum, a huge arena called an amphitheatre. It was used for staging games and fights, and first opened to the public in AD80.

TIMELINE 753BC–276BC

Rome's rise to power was sudden and spectacular. Its eventful history includes bloody battles, eccentric emperors, amazing inventions and remarkable feats of engineering. The Roman Empire prospered for almost 500 years, and still influences the way we live today.

Romulus, the first king of Rome

c.753BC The city of Rome is founded by Romulus, according to legend.

673–641BC Tullus Hostilius, Rome's third king, expands the city's territory by conquering a neighbouring settlement. Rome's population doubles as a result.

641–616BC Pons Sublicius, the first bridge across the river Tiber, is constructed. The harbour town of Ostia is founded at the mouth of the Tiber.

600BC The Latin language is first written in a script that is still used today.

inscription in Latin, carved in stone

750BC   700BC   650BC   600BC

CLUES TO THE PAST
The coin on this necklace dates from the reign of the Emperor Domitian, AD81–96. Gold does not rot like wood and other materials, so jewellery like this can give us clues about Roman craft methods, changing fashions, trade and even warfare.

SECRETS BENEATH THE SEA
Divers have discovered Roman shipwrecks deep under the waters of the Mediterranean Sea. Many have their cargo still intact. These jars were being transported over 2,000 years ago. By examining shipwrecks, archaeologists can learn how Roman boats were built, what they carried and where they traded.

ARCHAEOLOGISTS AT WORK
These archaeologists are excavating sections of wall plaster from the site of a Roman house in Britain. Many remains of Roman buildings and artefacts, as well as books and documents, have survived from that time. These all help us build up a picture of what life was like in the Roman Empire.

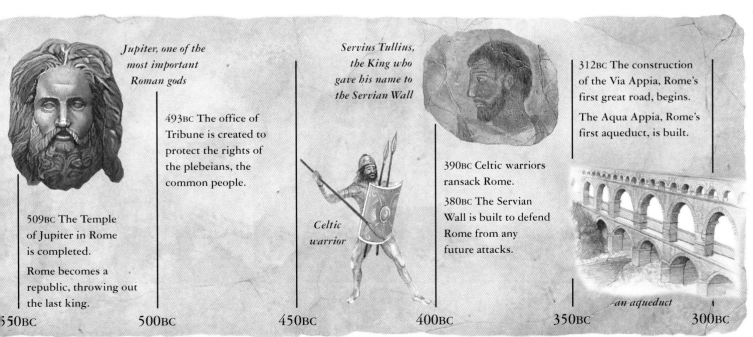

Jupiter, one of the most important Roman gods

Servius Tullius, the King who gave his name to the Servian Wall

312BC The construction of the Via Appia, Rome's first great road, begins.

The Aqua Appia, Rome's first aqueduct, is built.

493BC The office of Tribune is created to protect the rights of the plebeians, the common people.

390BC Celtic warriors ransack Rome.

380BC The Servian Wall is built to defend Rome from any future attacks.

Celtic warrior

509BC The Temple of Jupiter in Rome is completed.

Rome becomes a republic, throwing out the last king.

an aqueduct

550BC   500BC   450BC   400BC   350BC   300BC

The Great Empire

BRITAIN

London

FRANCE

SPAIN

B Y THE YEAR AD117, the Roman Empire was at its height. It was possible to travel 4,000km from east to west and still hear the trumpets of the Roman legions. As a Roman soldier you might have had to shiver in the snowy winters of northern Britain, or sweat and toil in the heat of the Egyptian desert.

The peoples of the Empire were very different. There were Greeks, Egyptians, Syrians, Jews, Africans, Germans and Celts. Many of them belonged to civilizations that were already ancient when Rome was still a group of villages. Many revolted against Roman rule, but uprisings were quickly put down. Gradually, conquered peoples came to accept being part of the Empire. From AD212 onwards, any free person living under Roman rule had the right to claim "I am a Roman citizen". Slaves, however, had very few rights.

In AD284, after a series of violent civil wars, this vast empire was divided into several parts. Despite being reunited by the Emperor Constantine in AD324, the Empire was doomed. A hundred years later, the western part was invaded by fierce warriors from the north, with disastrous consequences. Although the Western Empire came to an end in AD476, the eastern part continued until 1453. The Latin language survived, used by the Roman Catholic Church and by scientists and scholars across Europe. It is still learned today, and is the basis of languages such as Italian, Spanish, French and Romanian.

TIMELINE 275BC–1BC

264BC First record of a gladiatorial contest.

264-241BC The first of three wars between Rome and Carthage, which came to be known as the Punic Wars.

a gladiator

one of Hannibal's war elephants

250BC Rome controls most of Italy.

240BC The first Roman dramas are performed on stage.

218-201BC Second war between Rome and Carthage.

Hannibal, a Carthaginian general, crosses the Alps by elephant.

c.211BC The first Roman silver coin, *denarius*, is minted at Rome.

206BC Rome conquers Iberia (present-day Spain).

200BC The Romans are using concrete in buildings.

196BC Rome defeats the Macedonian rulers of Greece.

The first triumphal arches are built in Rome.

a triumphal arch, built to celebrate a victory

275BC   250BC   225BC   200BC   175BC

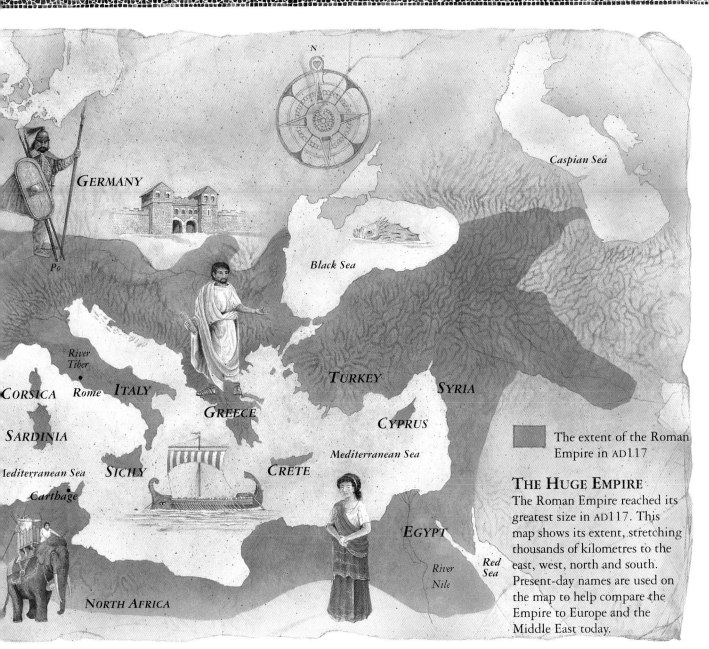

GERMANY

Po

Caspian Sea

Black Sea

River Tiber

CORSICA

Rome ITALY

TURKEY

SYRIA

GREECE

CYPRUS

SARDINIA

Mediterranean Sea

Mediterranean Sea SICILY CRETE

Carthage

EGYPT

River Nile

Red Sea

NORTH AFRICA

The extent of the Roman Empire in AD117

THE HUGE EMPIRE

The Roman Empire reached its greatest size in AD117. This map shows its extent, stretching thousands of kilometres to the east, west, north and south. Present-day names are used on the map to help compare the Empire to Europe and the Middle East today.

Roman soldiers armed for battle

slaves in chains

73BC Spartacus leads a slave revolt in southern Italy.

58-50BC Roman armies, led by Julius Caesar, conquer Gaul after a series of wars.

55BC Pompey's Theatre, the first stone-built theatre in Rome, is completed.

55-54BC Roman attacks on Britain begin.

a Roman open-air theatre

44BC Julius Caesar is murdered in the Senate.

31BC Battle of Actium – Octavian defeats Cleopatra of Egypt and Mark Antony, bringing an end to civil war.

29BC Egypt becomes part of the Roman Empire.

27BC Octavian becomes Rome's first emperor and is given the title Augustus.

149-146BC Third and final war between Rome and Carthage – Carthage is destroyed.

146BC Greece and North Africa come under Roman rule.

150BC   125BC   100BC   75BC   50BC   25BC

The Roman World

THE PEOPLE who made Roman history came from many different backgrounds. The names of the famous survive on monuments and in books. There were consuls and emperors, successful generals and powerful politicians, great writers and historians. However, it was thousands of ordinary people who really kept the Roman Empire going – merchants, soldiers of the legions, tax collectors, servants, farmers, potters, and others like them.

Many of the most famous names of that time were not Romans at all. There was the Carthaginian general, Hannibal, Rome's deadliest enemy. There were also Celtic chieftains and queens, such as Vercingetorix, Caractacus and Boudicca.

AUGUSTUS (63BC–AD14)
Augustus, born Octavian, was the great-nephew and adopted son of Julius Caesar. After Caesar's death, he took control of the army. He became ruler of the Roman world after defeating Mark Antony at the Battle of Actium in 31BC. In 27BC, he became Rome's first emperor and was given the title Augustus.

ROMULUS AND REMUS
According to legend, Romulus was the founder and first king of Rome. The legend tells how he and his twin brother Remus were abandoned as babies. They were saved by a she-wolf, who looked after them until they were found by a shepherd.

CICERO (106–43BC)
Cicero is remembered as Rome's greatest orator, or speaker. Many of his letters and speeches still survive. He was a writer, poet, politican, lawyer and philosopher. He was elected consul of Rome in 63BC, but he had many enemies and was murdered in 43BC.

TIMELINE AD1–AD476

c.AD30 Death of Jesus Christ.

AD43 The Roman conquest of Britain begins.

Boudicca, queen of the Iceni in Britain

AD50 Rome is the largest city in the world – population about 1 million.

Roman traders reach Bengal and India.

AD60 Queen Boudicca leads an uprising in Britain.

AD64 The Great Fire of Rome.

AD75 Roman traders reach the Sudan, setting up trade links across the Sahara.

AD79 The volcano Vesuvius erupts, burying Pompeii and Herculaneum.

AD80 The Colosseum in Rome is completed.

Vesuvius begins to erupt

AD117 The Roman Empire is at its largest.

AD118-128 The Pantheon in Rome is built.

AD122 Construction work begins on Hadrian's Wall, a defensive barrier across northern Britain.

the Pantheon in Rome

AD165-167 Plague spreads throughout the Empire.

cAD200 Road system covers all parts of the Empire.

AD212 All free people in the Empire are granted citizenship.

AD1　　　AD50　　　AD100　　　AD150　　　AD200

HADRIAN (AD76–138)
Hadrian became emperor in AD117 and spent many years travelling around the Empire. He had many splendid buildings constructed, as well as a defensive barrier across northern Britain, now known as Hadrian's Wall.

NERO (AD37–68) AND AGRIPPINA
Nero became emperor on the death of his adoptive father Claudius, in AD54. A cruel ruler, he was blamed for a great fire that destroyed much of Rome in AD64. Agrippina, his mother, was a powerful influence on him. She was suspected of poisoning two of her three husbands, and was eventually killed on her son's orders.

CLEOPATRA (68–30BC)
An Egyptian queen of Greek descent, Cleopatra had a son by Julius Caesar. She then fell in love with Mark Antony, a close follower of Caesar. They joined forces against Rome, but after a crushing defeat at Actium in 31BC, they both committed suicide. Egypt then became part of the Roman Empire.

JULIUS CAESAR (100–44BC)
Caesar was a talented and popular general and politician. He led Roman armies in an eight-year campaign to conquer Gaul (present-day France) in 50BC. In 49BC, he used his victorious troops to seize power and declare himself dictator for life. Five years later he was stabbed to death in the Senate by fellow politicians.

---

the cross, a symbol of Christianity

AD270 A new defensive wall is built around Rome by the Emperor Aurelian.

AD284 The Emperor Diocletian brings in new laws and taxes – divisions appear in the Empire.

AD313 Christianity is made legal in the Empire.

AD324 The Emperor Constantine reunites the Empire and founds the city of Constantinople (present-day Istanbul, in Turkey).

AD330 Constantine makes Constantinople his imperial residence and the new capital in the east.

AD395 The Roman Empire is divided again, this time into two parts – Eastern and Western.

the Emperor Constantine, depicted on a Roman coin

AD410 The city of Rome is raided and ransacked by Visigoth armies from Germany.

Vandal warrior

AD455 Vandal armies from Germany ransack Rome.

AD476 Fall of the Western Empire – the Eastern Empire survives until 1453.

AD250	AD300	AD350	AD400	AD450

Rulers of Rome

IN THE EARLY DAYS, the city of Rome was ruled by kings. The first Roman king was said to be Romulus, the founder of the city in 753BC. The last king, a hated tyrant called Tarquinius the Proud, was thrown out in 509BC. The Romans then set up a republic. An assembly of powerful and wealthy citizens, the Senate, chose two consuls to lead them each year. By 493BC, the common people had their own representatives, too – the tribunes. In times of crisis, rulers could take on emergency powers and become dictators. The first Roman emperor, Augustus, was appointed by the Senate in 27BC. The emperors were given great powers and were even worshipped as gods. Some lived simply and ruled well, but others were violent, cruel men. They were surrounded by flatterers, and yet they lived in constant fear of plotters and murderers.

TRIUMPHAL PROCESSION
When a Roman general won a great victory, he was honoured with a military parade called a triumph. Cheering crowds lined the streets as the grand procession passed by. If a general was successful and popular, the way to power was often open to him. Probably the most famous Roman ruler of all, Julius Caesar, came to power after a series of brilliant military conquests.

STATE SACRIFICE
Roman emperors had religious as well as political duties. As *pontifex maximus*, or high priest, an emperor would make sacrifices as offerings to the gods at important festivals.

figs

DEADLY FRUIT

Who killed Augustus, the first Roman emperor, in AD14? It was hard to say. It might have been a natural death... but then again, it might have been caused by his wife Livia. She was said to have coated the figs in his garden with a deadly poison. Roman emperors were much feared, but they were surrounded by enemies and could trust no one, least of all their own families.

PRAETORIAN GUARDS

The Praetorian Guards were the emperor's personal bodyguards. They wore special uniforms and were well paid. The guards were the only armed soldiers allowed within the city of Rome and so became very powerful. They also intervened in politics – assassinating the Emperor Caligula and electing his successor, Claudius.

In Rome, wreaths made from leaves of the laurel tree were worn by emperors, victorious soldiers and athletes. The wreath was a badge of honour. The Romans copied the idea from the ancient Greeks.

WREATH OF HONOUR

You will need: tape measure, garden wire, pliers, scissors, clear tape, green ribbon, bay or laurel leaves (real or fake).

1 Measure around your head with the tape measure. Cut some wire the same length, so the wreath will fit you. Bend the wire as shown and tape the ribbon round it.

2 Start to tape the leaves by their stems on to the wire, as shown above. Work your way around to the middle of the wire, fanning out the leaves as you go.

3 Then reverse the direction of the leaves and work your way around the rest of the wire. Fit the finished wreath to your head. Hail, Caesar!

Roman Society

ROMAN SOCIETY was never very fair. At first, a group of rich and powerful noble families, called the patricians, controlled the city and the Senate. Anyone who wanted their voice heard had to persuade a senator to speak on their behalf. Over the centuries the common citizens, known as plebeians, became more powerful until, by 287BC, they shared equally in government. Eventually, in the days of the Empire, even people of humble birth could become emperor, provided they were wealthy or had the support of the army. Emperors always feared riots by the common people of Rome, so they tried to keep the people happy with handouts of free food and lavish entertainments. Roman women had little power outside the family and could not vote. However, many were successful in business or had an important influence on political events. Slaves had very few rights, though Roman society depended on slave labour. Prisoners of war were bought and sold as slaves and many were treated cruelly, making slave revolts common.

A ROMAN CONSUL
This is a statue of a Roman consul, or leader of the Senate, in the days of the republic. At first, only the noble, and often wealthy, ruling class could be senators. However, under the emperors, the power and influence of the Senate slowly grew less and less.

LIFE AS A SLAVE
The everyday running of the Empire depended on slavery. This mosaic shows a young slave boy carrying fruit. In about AD100, a wealthy family might have had as many as 500 slaves. Some families treated their slaves well, and slaves who gave good service might earn their freedom. However, many more led miserable lives, toiling in the mines or labouring in the fields.

SLAVE TAG
This bronze disc was probably worn around the neck of a slave, like a dog-tag. The Latin words on it say: "Hold me, in case I run away, and return me to my master Viventius on the estate of Callistus". Slaves had few rights and could be branded on the forehead or leg as the property of their owners.

COLLECTING TAXES

This stone carving probably shows people paying their annual taxes. Officials counted the population of the Empire and registered them for paying tax. Money from taxes paid for the army and the government. However, many of the tax collectors took bribes, and even emperors seized public money to add to their private fortunes.

ARISTOCRATS

This Italian painting of the 1700s imagines how a noble Roman lady might dress after bathing. Wealthy people had personal slaves to help them bathe, dress and look after their hair. Household slaves were sometimes almost part of the family, and their children might be brought up and educated with their owner's children.

Country Life

THE FIRST ROMANS mostly lived by farming. Even when Rome had become a big city, Roman poets still liked to sing the praises of the countryside. In reality, country life was quite hard. Oxen were used for ploughing. Grain crops were harvested with a sickle, and flour was often ground by hand. Water had to be fetched by hand from the farm's well or a nearby spring.

Many farms were very small. They were often run by retired soldiers, who would raise chickens and geese and perhaps a cow or pig. They would also keep bees and grow olives and a few vegetables.

Other farms in Italy and across the Empire were large estates set up to provide incomes for their wealthy landowners. These estates might have their own olive presses, reaping machines and stores for drying grain. An estate was often laid out around a large, luxurious house or villa. Other villas were grand country houses owned by rich and powerful Romans.

A COUNTRY ESTATE
Life on a country estate was always busy, as this mosaic of a Roman villa in Tunisia, North Africa, shows. North African country estates supplied Rome with vast amounts of grain, fruit and vegetables. The good soil, combined with hot summers and rain in winter, made farming easy.

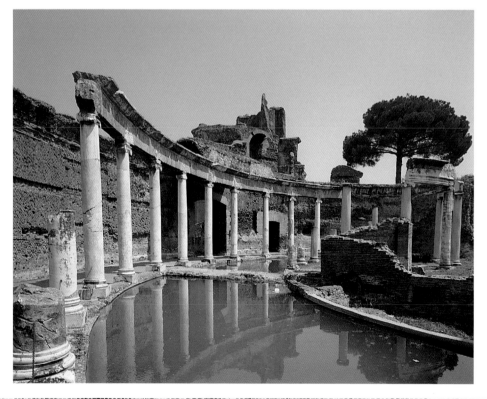

HADRIAN'S VILLA
One of the grandest country houses of all was built for the Emperor Hadrian between AD124 and 133. Parts of the villa still stand today, as this view of one of its lakeside walks shows. The luxurious villa itself stood on a hilltop, with Rome just visible in the distance. Built on land that belonged to Hadrian's family, the villa had pavilions and pools, terraces, banqueting halls, theatres and libraries. All around the villa were parklands filled with trees, such as laurels, planes and pines, exotic shrubs and formal flowerbeds. Hadrian designed the villa as a holiday palace where he could escape from the cares of government, but he died just four years after it was completed.

HUNTING WILD BOAR

Hunting scenes often decorated the walls of country villas. The hunt was a favourite pastime for young noblemen or army officers visiting the countryside. A wild boar, like the one shown in this mosaic, was one of the most dangerous animals of all when it charged.

FOOD FOR ROME

Rome needed huge amounts of food for all its people. Vegetables, such as leeks, celery, cabbage, beans and peas, were grown at market gardens around the city. Grain crops included wheat, barley, oats and rye. Grapes were made into wine and, as there was no sugar, honey was used to sweeten foods.

grapes

wheat

honey

GROVES OF OLIVE TREES

Olives were, and still are, an important crop in the lands around the Mediterranean. They were grown on small farms as well as on large estates. The oil was pressed and stored in large pottery jars. It was used for cooking or burnt in oil lamps.

PLOUGHING THE LAND

This ploughman from Roman Britain is using a heavy wooden plough drawn by oxen. Large areas of Europe were still covered in thick forest in the days of the Roman Empire. Gradually farmers cleared land to plough, and farmland and orchards spread across the countryside.

Town and City

MANY OF THE TOWNS in Italy and the lands surrounding the Mediterranean Sea were already old and well-established when the Romans invaded. Under Roman rule these towns prospered and grew. In other parts of Europe, where people had never lived in a big town, the Roman invaders built impressive new cities.

Roman towns had straight, paved roads planned on a grid pattern. Some were broad streets with pavements. Others were alleys just wide enough for a donkey. Most streets were busy with noisy crowds, street merchants, carts and rowdy bars. The streets divided the buildings into blocks called *insulae*, which means islands. The homes of wealthy families were spacious and comfortable. Poorer Romans often lived in apartment blocks that were badly built, crowded and in constant danger of burning down.

Fresh water was brought into towns through a system of channels called an aqueduct. The water was piped to fountains, public baths and to the homes of the wealthy.

On August 24, AD79, the volcano Vesuvius erupted violently, burying the Roman town of Pompeii in ash and lava. Work began in 1748 to excavate the ancient town, and its streets, shops and houses have slowly been revealed. In this excavated street, the deep ruts in the road made by cart wheels are clearly visible. Streets were often filled with mud and filth, so stepping-stones were laid for pedestrians to cross.

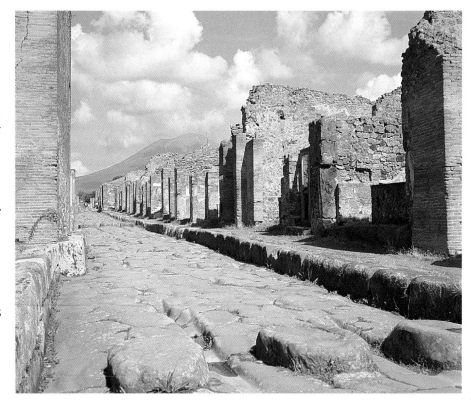

AN AQUEDUCT BRIDGE

You will need: ruler, pencil, scissors, thick and thin card, PVA glue, paintbrush, masking tape, modelling clay, plaster paste, acrylic paints, water pot.

37cm

3.5cm

40.5cm

10.5cm

7.5cm   2.5cm   1.5cm

41.5cm

10.5cm

7.5cm   2.5cm   2cm

Cut out pieces of card following the measurements shown.

1 Draw and cut out the shapes of the arches from the thick card. You need to cut out a pair for each level of the aqueduct – top, middle and bottom.

AQUEDUCTS

Water was carried into Roman towns and cities through a system of channels and pipes called aqueducts. Most of these were underground. Sometimes they were supported on high arches, such as this one, which still stands today in France. The water came from fresh springs, streams and lakes.

HERCULANEUM

The volcanic eruption that buried Pompeii caused a mud flow that buried a nearby coastal town, Herculaneum. Here, too, archaeologists have discovered houses, public baths, shops and workshops side by side on the city's streets. This view shows how crowded parts of the town were, with narrow paved streets separating the buildings.

CITY PLAN

This aerial view of Pompeii clearly shows how Roman streets were laid out on a grid pattern.

Forum baths

Stabian baths

amphitheatre

sports ground

N

large theatre

market

Capitol

Forum

0	200	400m
0	200	400yds

Aqueducts were built at a slight slope to ensure a steady flow of water. Arched bridges carried them across river valleys. The water flowed along a channel at the top of the bridge.

2 Cut strips of thin card in three widths – 4cm, 2.5cm and 2cm. These are for the insides of the arches. Use glue and tape to fix the 4cm strips to the bottom level.

3 Glue on the other side of the bottom level. Fix it securely with tape. Cut a top section from thick card and fix this on. Make the two other levels in the same way.

4 Roll the modelling clay into buttresses and wrap with thick card. Attach these to the three central arches of the bottom level. These will support the aqueduct bridge.

5 Glue the levels together. Cover the model with plaster paste and mark on a brick pattern. Leave to dry. Paint the arches grey. Paint a blue channel of 'water' on top.

House and Garden

ONLY WEALTHY ROMANS could afford to live in a private house. A typical town house was designed to look inwards, with the rooms arranged round a central courtyard and a walled garden. Outside walls had few windows and these were small and shuttered. The front door opened on to a short passage leading into an airy courtyard called an *atrium*. Front rooms on either side of the passage were usually used as bedrooms. Sometimes they were used as workshops or shops, having shutters that opened out to the street.

The centre of the atrium was open to the sky. Below this opening was a pool, set into the floor, to collect rainwater. Around the atrium were more bedrooms and the kitchen. If you were a guest or had important business you would be shown into the *tablinium*. The dining room, or *triclinium*, was often the grandest room of all. The very rich sometimes also had a summer dining room, which looked on to the garden.

Houses were made of locally available building materials. These might include stone, mud bricks, cement and timber. Roofs were made of clay tiles.

garden

bedroom

tablinium (living room and office)

LOCKS AND KEYS
This was the key to the door of a Roman house. Pushed in through a keyhole, the prongs at the end of the key fitted into holes in the bolt in the lock. The key could then be used to slide the bolt along and unlock the door.

INSIDE A ROMAN HOME
The outside of a wealthy Roman's town house was usually quite plain, but inside it was highly decorated with elaborate wall paintings and intricate mosaics. The rooms were sparsely furnished, with couches or beds, small side tables, benches and folding stools. There were few windows, but high ceilings and wide doors made the most of the light from the open atrium and the garden.

MAKE A ROMAN HOME
You will need: pencil, ruler, thick card, scissors, PVA glue, paintbrushes, masking tape, corrugated cardboard, thin card, water pot, acrylic paints.

7.5cm   7.5cm
15cm
15cm   23cm   10cm
53cm   57cm
30cm
26cm   26cm   26cm   15cm
15cm   10cm   x 2   15cm   26cm   10cm   x 2

Cut out pieces of card following the measurements shown.

water spout

atrium
(courtyard)

bedroom

triclinium
(dining room)

kitchen

GARDEN DELIGHTS
At the back of many Roman houses lay beautiful, walled gardens with stone columns, pools, fountains, statues and terraces. People would eat out here on warm evenings, reclining on couches and surrounded by trailing ivy, sweet-smelling roses, irises, lilies, bay trees and cypresses.

ivy

roses

This Roman house has high, windowless walls to shut out the hot summer sun, making it cool and shady inside.

1 Cut out the pieces of thick card. Edge each piece with glue. Press the pieces together and reinforce with masking tape, as shown. You have now made the walls of your house.

2 Measure your model and cut out pieces of corrugated cardboard for the roofs. Stick them together with glue, as shown above. Paint the roofs red.

3 Rainwater running down the sloped atrium roof was directed into a pool below by gutters and water spouts. Make gutters from strips of thin card, with holes as spouts.

4 Paint the house walls as shown, using masking tape to get a straight line. Glue on the roofs. Why not finish off your Roman house with some authentic graffiti!

Home Comforts

ROMAN HOUSES were less cluttered with furniture than our own. People kept their clothes in cupboards and wooden chests rather than in wardrobes or drawers. Wooden or metal stools were used more than chairs. Couches were the most important piece of furniture, used for resting, eating and receiving visitors. Roman furniture was often simple, but rich people could afford fine, hand-crafted tables or benches made from wood, marble or bronze. Dining tables were very low, because wealthy Romans ate their evening meal lying on couches. Beds were often made of wood, with slats or ropes to support the mattress and pillows, which were stuffed with wool or straw.

Lighting in both rich and poor homes came from many small, flickering oil lamps made from clay or bronze. Heating came from charcoal burned in open braziers. The most luxurious houses were warmed by underfloor central heating, especially in colder parts of the Empire.

INTERIOR DECORATION
The walls, ceilings and floors of Roman houses were covered with paintings, mosaics and moulded plaster reliefs. Elaborate scenes were painted directly on to the walls, while bright patterns in tiles and mosaics decorated the floor.

A HYPOCAUST
Roman underfloor heating is called a hypocaust. These are the remains of the hypocaust at the palace of Fishbourne in England. Only wealthy Romans could afford this early form of central heating, and many only had it in the dining room.

UNDERFLOOR HEATING
A furnace, burning wood or charcoal, heated the air beneath the floor. The hot air circulated around pillars of brick or tile that supported the floor. It also flowed up inside the walls through special channels. This kept the whole room warm. Slaves would keep the furnace stoked up.

mosaic-covered floor warmed from below

outside furnace with stokehole at front

hot air from the furnace flows under the floor and up inside the walls

HOUSEHOLD SHRINE

The *lararium*, or household shrine, was a small private altar containing images of the family's ancestors. It was usually situated in the *atrium* at the centre of the house. Every day the family would honour their ancestors by burning incense at the shrine.

DINNER IS SERVED

These are guests at a banquet in Roman Germany. Only country folk, foreigners and slaves ate sitting upright at the table. Tables and chairs were usually made of wood and might be carved or painted. There were also woven wicker armchairs. Wealthy Romans ate lying on couches around a central low table.

LAMPLIGHT

Roman homes glowed with the soft light of candles and oil lamps. Lamps were made of pottery or bronze, like this one. They came in many different designs, but they all had a central well containing olive oil. The oil was soaked up by a wick, which provided a steady flame. Sometimes lamps would be grouped together or hung from a tall lampstand.

A LUXURY TO LIE ON

This beautifully decorated bed is made from wood inlaid with ivory and semi-precious stones. It dates back to about 50BC, and was discovered in the remains of a villa in Italy. The villa had been buried under ash from a volcanic eruption. Beds, or couches for sleeping on, were much higher than ours are today and needed steps or a stool to get on to.

In the Kitchen

WHEN A LARGE MEAL was being prepared, slaves would have to carry water and fresh kindling for the fire into the kitchen. As the fires were lit, the room would become quite smoky because there was no chimney. Soon the coals would be glowing red hot and pots would be boiling on trivets and griddles on the raised brick stove. Food was boiled, fried, grilled and stewed. Larger kitchens might include stone ovens for baking bread or spits for roasting meat. A few even had piped hot water.

The kitchens of wealthy Romans were well equipped with all kinds of bronze pots, pans, strainers and ladles. Pottery storage jars held wine, olive oil and sauces. Herbs, vegetables and joints of meat hung from hooks in the roof. There were no tins, and no fridges or freezers to keep food fresh. Food had to be preserved in oil or by drying, smoking, salting or pickling.

mortar

VALUABLE GLASS
This glass bottle or jug was made about 1,900 years ago. Precious liquids or expensive perfumes were sold in bottles like this throughout the Empire. When a bottle was empty, it was far too valuable to throw away, so it was often reused to store food such as honey in the kitchen.

pestle

PESTLE AND MORTAR
The Romans liked spicy food. Roman cooks used a pestle and mortar to grind up foods, such as nuts, herbs and spices, into a paste. Both pieces were usually made of a very tough pottery or stone. The rough inside of the mortar was made of coarse grit to help grind the food.

A ROMAN KITCHEN

You will need: pencil, ruler, cardboard, scissors, paintbrush, PVA glue, masking tape, water pot, acrylic paints, red felt tip pen, plaster paste, balsa wood, sandpaper, self-drying clay, work board, modelling tool.

1 Cut out the walls and floor of the kitchen from cardboard, as shown. Glue the edges and press them together. Reinforce the walls with pieces of masking tape.

2 Paint the floor grey. When dry, use the ruler and pencil to draw on stone flags. Paint the walls yellow, edged with blue. When dry, use the felt tip to draw stripes.

3 Cut out pieces of card to make a stove about 2cm long, 5cm wide and 4cm high. Glue the pieces together and reinforce with masking tape, as shown above.

READY FOR THE COOK

Herbs brought fresh from the garden included coriander, oregano, rue, mint, thyme and parsley. Food was spiced with pepper, caraway, aniseed, mustard seeds and saffron. On the table there might be eggs, grapes, figs and nuts. Much of our knowledge of Roman cooking comes from recipes collected by a Roman gourmet called Apicius nearly 2,000 years ago.

saffron

thyme

mint

quails' eggs

BAKING PAN

This bronze tray was probably used as a mould for baking honey cakes, buns or pastries. The long handle makes it easier to remove from a hot oven. It may also have been used to cook eggs.

STRAINER

This bronze strainer was used by Roman cooks to strain sauces. It was made using the same design as a saucepan, but its bowl has been pierced with an intricate pattern. The hole in the handle was used to hang it from a hook on the wall.

SAUCEPAN

Like many Roman kitchen utensils, this saucepan is made from bronze. Bronze contains copper, which can give food a very strange flavour – the inside of the saucepan has been coated with silver to prevent this from happening.

Foods in a Roman kitchen were stored in baskets, bowls or sacks. Wine, oil and sauces were stored in pottery jars called amphorae.

4 Coat the stove with plaster paste. Leave to dry. Then use sandpaper to rub it smooth. Make a grate from two strips of card and four bits of balsa wood, glued together.

5 Use the acrylic paints to colour the stove and the grate, as shown above. Use small pieces of balsa wood to make a pile of wood fuel to store underneath the stove.

6 Make a table and shelves from balsa wood, as shown. Glue them together, and bind with masking tape. Leave them to dry before painting the pieces brown.

7 Use the clay to model pots, pans, bowls, storage jars, perhaps even a frying pan or an egg poacher. Leave the utensils to dry before painting them a suitable colour.

Food and Drink

FOR POOR ROMANS, a meal was often little more than a hurried bowl of porridge or a crust of bread washed down with sour wine. Many town-dwellers lived in homes without kitchens. They ate takeaway meals bought from the many food stalls and bars in town. Even for wealthier people, breakfast might be just a quick snack of bread, honey and olives. Lunch, too, was a light meal, perhaps of eggs or cold meats and fruit. The main meal of the day was *cena*, or dinner. This evening meal might start with shellfish or a salad, followed by a main course of roast meat, such as pork, veal, chicken or goose, with vegetables. It finished with a sweet course of fruit or honey cakes.

More lavish banquets might include fattened dormice, songbirds, flamingoes' tongues or a custard made from calves' brains and rose hips! Food was heavily spiced and was often served with a fish sauce called *garum*. Wine was usually mixed with water and sometimes flavoured with honey or spices. Guests could take home any tasty morsels that were left over.

SERVING SLAVES
This mosaic shows a slave called Paregorius helping to prepare his master's table for a banquet. On his head he is carrying a tray with plates of food. During a banquet, dishes were brought in a few at a time and set down on a small table. All the food was cooked and served by slaves.

HONEYED DATES
You will need: chopping board, dates, small knife, walnuts, pecan nuts, almonds, hazelnuts, pestle and mortar, salt, 175ml honey, frying pan, wooden spoon, a few fresh mint leaves.

1 On the chopping board, slit open the dates with the knife. Remove the stone inside. Be sure not to cut the dates completely in half and be careful with the knife.

2 Put aside the hazelnuts. Chop up the rest of the nuts. Use a pestle and mortar to grind them into smaller pieces. Stuff a small amount into the middle of each date.

3 Pour some salt on to the chopping board and lightly roll each date in it. Make sure the dates are coated all over, but do not use too much salt.

CUPS

Pottery cups like this one were used for drinking wine. Many drinking cups had handles and were often highly decorated. Metal cups could make wine taste unpleasant, so coloured glass cups and pottery cups were more popular.

THE FAMILY SILVER

These silver spoons were used by a wealthy family in Roman Britain. Food was usually eaten with the fingers, but spoons were used for sauces. At banquets, Romans liked to bring out their best silver tableware as a sign of status.

AT A BANQUET

This wall painting shows a typical Roman banquet. Guests usually sat three to a couch. After the meal they were entertained with poetry readings and music, or jokes and jugglers. Dress and table manners were very important at a banquet. Arguments and bad language were not allowed, but it was fine to spit, belch or even eat until you were sick!

4 On a low heat, melt the honey in the frying pan. Lightly fry the dates for five minutes, turning them with a wooden spoon. Take care while using the stove.

5 Arrange the stuffed dates in a shallow dish. Sprinkle over the whole hazelnuts, some chopped nuts and a few leaves of fresh mint. Now they are ready to serve to your friends.

The Romans loved sweet dishes made from nuts and dates imported from North Africa. They also used dates to make sauces for savoury dishes such as fish and roast duck.

Getting Dressed

OST ROMAN CLOTHES were made of wool that had been spun and woven by hand at home or in a workshop. Flax was grown in Egypt to make linen, while cotton from India and silk from China were rare and expensive imports. The most common style of clothing was a simple tunic, which was practical for people who led active lives, such as workers, slaves and children. Important men also wore a white robe called a toga. This was a 6m length of cloth with a curved edge, wrapped around the body and draped over the shoulder. It was heavy and uncomfortable to wear, but looked very impressive. Women wore a long dress called a *stola*, over an under-tunic. Often they also wore a *palla* – a large shawl that could be arranged in various ways. Girls wore white until they were married, after which they often wore dresses dyed in bright colours.

ROMAN FOOTWEAR
This sandal (*left*) and child's shoe (*far left*) were found in York, in Britain. Most Romans wore open leather sandals. There were many different designs, and some had nailed soles to make them harder wearing. Shoes and boots were worn in the colder parts of the Empire.

DRESSING FOR DIONYSUS
Wall paintings in the homes of wealthy Romans hold many clues about the way people dressed in the Roman world. This scene was found in the Villa of the Mysteries, in Pompeii. It shows young women being prepared as ceremonial brides for Dionysus, the god of wine.

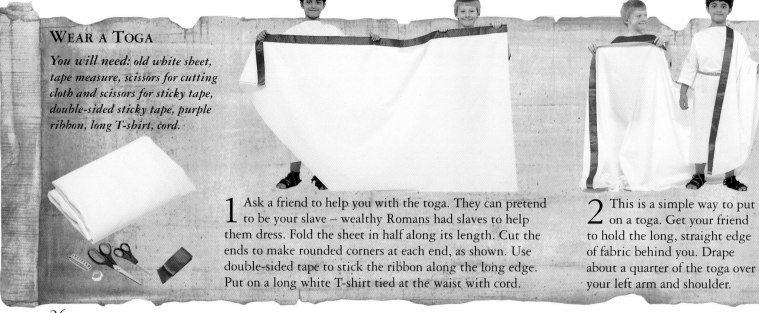

WEAR A TOGA
You will need: old white sheet, tape measure, scissors for cutting cloth and scissors for sticky tape, double-sided sticky tape, purple ribbon, long T-shirt, cord.

1 Ask a friend to help you with the toga. They can pretend to be your slave – wealthy Romans had slaves to help them dress. Fold the sheet in half along its length. Cut the ends to make rounded corners at each end, as shown. Use double-sided tape to stick the ribbon along the long edge. Put on a long white T-shirt tied at the waist with cord.

2 This is a simple way to put on a toga. Get your friend to hold the long, straight edge of fabric behind you. Drape about a quarter of the toga over your left arm and shoulder.

WORKERS' CLOTHES

Not all Romans wore flowing robes. This man is probably a farm worker from Roman Germany. He wears strips of cloth around his legs and a hooded leather cloak to protect him from the cold, wet weather. Hooded cloaks like this were exported from Gaul (present-day France) and Britain.

DRESSED TO IMPRESS

This stone carving shows the family of the Emperor Augustus, dressed for an important state occasion. The women are all shown wearing a *stola*, with a *palla* draped round their shoulders or head. The men and boys are shown in togas. A toga could be worn by all free Roman citizens, but only the wealthy upper classes wore it. This was because it took time – and a helping hand – to put on a toga. Once you had it on, it was also quite awkward to move in!

3 Bring the rest of the toga round to the front, passing it under your right arm. Hook the toga up by tucking a few folds of material securely into the cord around your waist.

4 Now your friend can help you fold the rest of the toga neatly over your left arm, as shown above. If you prefer, you could drape it all over your left shoulder.

Boys from wealthy families wore togas edged with a thin purple stripe until they reached the age of 16. They then wore plain togas. A toga with a broad purple stripe was worn by Roman senators. Purple dye was expensive, so the colour was only worn by high-ranking citizens.

Fashion and Beauty

A ROMAN LADY would spend most of the morning surrounded by her female slaves. Some would bring her a mirror made of bronze or silver and jars of perfumed oils or ointments. Another slave would comb out her hair – and could expect a spiteful jab with a hairpin if she pulled at a tangle.

Most rich women wanted to look pale – after all, only women who had to work outdoors became sunburnt. So chalk, or even a poisonous powder made from white lead, was rubbed into the face. Face packs were made of bread and milk. One remedy for spots and pimples included bird droppings! Lipsticks and blusher were made of red ochre or the sediment from red wine. Eyeshadow was made of ash and saffron. Women's hair was curled, plaited or pinned up, according to the latest fashion.

PORTRAIT OF A LADY
This is a portrait of a lady who lived in the Roman province of Egypt. Her earrings and necklace are made of emeralds, garnets and pearls set in gold. They are a sign of her wealth as they would have been very expensive. Her hair has been curled, and lamp-black or soot may have been used to darken her eyelashes and eyebrows.

CARVED COMB
This comb is carved from ivory and is inscribed in Latin with the words "Modestina farewell". Combs of silver and ivory were used to decorate the intricate hairstyles favoured by many Roman women. The poor used wooden or bone combs, though more out of need than fashion.

SCENT BOTTLES
These lovely perfume bottles belonged to a Roman lady. The round one is made of hand-blown, gold-banded glass. The other is carved from onyx, a precious stone with layers of different colours.

A GOLDEN HEADDRESS
You will need: tape measure, plain card, pencil, scissors, PVA glue, paintbrush, string, plastic beads, gold foil wrappers, sticky tape or paper clip.

1 Measure around your head with the tape measure. Draw the shape of the tiara to the same length on card. Also draw outlines for various sizes of leaf shape, as shown.

2 Carefully cut out the tiara outline from the card. Also cut out the leaf shapes. Then cut out the centre of each one so that they look a bit like arches.

3 Use the PVA glue and a paintbrush to paste the shapes securely on to the front of the tiara. These will be part of an elegant pattern for your tiara.

CROWNING GLORY

This lady's elaborately curled hair is almost certainly a wig. Hairpieces and wigs were always popular with wealthy Roman women– a bride would wear at least six pads of artificial hair at her wedding. Locks of black hair were usually imported from Asia, while blond or red hair came from northern Europe.

MEN'S CHANGING HAIRSTYLES

Roman men were just as concerned with their appearance as women. They usually wore their hair short, either combed forward or curled. They were mostly clean shaven, but beards became fashionable during the reign of the Emperor Hadrian, AD117–138.

A FINE DISPLAY

This picture shows a ceremonial dance at the Temple of the Sun in Rome. Both the men and women are wearing golden headdresses decorated with precious jewels and gold filigree. Lavish displays like this were reserved for grand public occasions to show off the wealth and power of the Empire.

RINGS ON THEIR FINGERS

Both men and women wore jewellery, especially rings. Rich people would wear rings like these, usually made of gold or silver. Emeralds, pearls and amber were also used in rings. The less wealthy would wear rings of bronze.

4 Cut lengths of string and glue them around the inside edges of the shapes. Glue plastic beads at the top of each arch, so that they look like precious stones.

5 Collect gold foil from sweet wrappers and glue it on to the tiara. Use the end of the paintbrush to carefully poke the foil into all the corners around the beads.

The finished tiara can be held together at the back by tape or a clip. Roman ladies liked to wear tiaras made of gold, with jewels in their hair.

Lessons and Learning

MOST CHILDREN in the Roman Empire never went to school. They learned a trade from their parents or found out about sums by trading on a market stall. Boys might be trained to fight with swords or to ride horses, in preparation for joining the army. Girls would be taught how to run the home, in preparation for marriage.

Wealthy families did provide an education for their sons and sometimes for their daughters, too. They were usually taught at home by a private tutor, but there were also small schools. Tutors and schoolmasters would teach children arithmetic, and how to read and write in both Latin and Greek. Clever pupils might also learn public speaking skills, poetry and history. Girls often had music lessons at home, on a harp-like instrument called a lyre.

INKPOTS AND PENS
Pen and ink were used to write on scrolls made from papyrus (a kind of reed) or thin sheets of wood. Ink was often made from soot or lamp-black, mixed with water. It was kept in inkpots such as these. Inkpots were made from glass, pottery or metal. Pens were made from bone, reeds or bronze.

WRITING IN WAX
This painting shows a couple from Pompeii. The man holds a parchment scroll. His wife is probably going through their household accounts. She holds a wax-covered writing tablet and a stylus to scratch words into the wax. A stylus had a pointed end for writing and a flat end for rubbing out.

A WRITING TABLET
You will need: sheets and sticks of balsa wood, craft knife, ruler, PVA glue, paintbrush, brown acrylic paint, water pot, modelling clay, work board, rolling pin, modelling tool, skewer, purple thread, pencil (to be used as a stylus), gold paint.

1 Use the craft knife to cut the balsa sheet into two rectangles 10cm x 22cm. The sticks of balsa should be cut into four lengths 22cm long and four lengths 10cm long.

2 Glue the sticks around the edges of each sheet as shown. These form a shallow hollow into which you can press the 'wax'. Paint the two frames a rich brown colour.

3 Roll out the modelling clay on a board and place a balsa frame on top. Use the modelling tool to cut around the outside of the frame. Repeat this step.

WRITING IT DOWN

Various materials were used for writing. Melted beeswax was poured into wooden trays to make writing tablets. Letters were scratched into the wax, which could be used again and again. Powdered soot was mixed with water and other ingredients to make ink for writing on papyrus, parchment or wood.

soot

melted beeswax

Roman numerals on papyrus

TEACHER AND PUPILS

This stone sculpture from Roman Germany shows a teacher seated between two of his pupils. They are reading their lessons from papyrus scrolls. Children had to learn poetry and other writings by heart. Any bad behaviour or mistakes were punished with a beating.

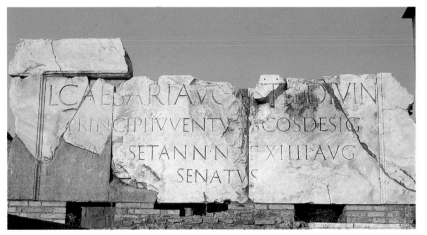

LETTERS IN STONE

Temples, monuments and public buildings were covered in Latin inscriptions, such as this one. Each letter was beautifully chiselled by a stonemason. These words are carved in marble. The inscription marked the 14th birthday of Lucius Caesar, the grandson of the Emperor Augustus.

4 Cut off about 1cm all around the edge of each modelling clay rectangle. This helps to make sure that the modelling clay will fit inside the balsa wood frame.

5 Carefully press the clay into each side – this represents the wax. Use the skewer to poke two holes through the inside edge of each frame, as shown.

6 Join the two frames together by threading purple thread through each pair of holes and tying it securely together. You have now made your tablet.

Paint the pencil gold to make it look as if it is made of metal. Use it like a stylus to scratch words on your tablet. Why not try writing in Latin? You could write CIVIS ROMANVS SVM, which means "I am a Roman citizen".

In the Forum

EVERY LARGE ROMAN TOWN had a forum – a market square with
public buildings around it. This was where people gathered to
do business and exchange friendly gossip. In the morning, while the
lady of the house had her hair done and her children struggled with
their lessons, her husband would walk over to the forum.

In the forum's central square, crowds thronged around market stalls.
Sometimes a public row might break out as inspectors of weights and
measures accused some trader of cheating his customers. Around the
square were shops, imposing monuments, marble statues and temples
to the gods. The walls of buildings were often scrawled with graffiti
made up of political messages, personal insults or declarations of love.
On one side of the forum was the basilica, a large building used as the
town hall, a law court and public
meeting place. Some of the crowds
may have been members of
the *curia* or town council,
or one of the trade guilds
who had their halls there.

DOWNTOWN POMPEII
The ruins at Pompeii include these
remains of a row of columns. They
were part of a two-storey colonnade
that once took up three sides of the
forum. Rows of shops and market
stalls were set up behind the
colonnade at ground level.

TEMPLES AND PROSPERITY
The forum of every town had splendid
temples to the many gods and goddesses of
ancient Rome. There were also temples for
famous Romans. The grand columns of this
temple still remain in the forum at Rome.
Today, a Christian church stands behind
it. The temple was built in honour of
Antoninus Pius, one of Rome's wisest
emperors, and his wife Faustina.

MAKING MONEY

Money changers and bankers gathered to make deals and discuss business in the forum. Here, too, tax collectors raised money for the town council – taxes were charged on all goods that passed through the town.

FAST FOOD

As people hurried to work or chatted with friends, they might pick up a snack from a food stall or a street vendor. Pastries filled with spicy meats made popular snacks. On market day, the forum would also be busy with traders and farmers setting up stalls in the central square.

THE BASILICA

This is the Basilica of Maxentius in Rome. A basilica was a huge building used as a cross between a town hall and law courts. It usually had a very high roof, supported by rows of columns. The columns divided the building into a central area with two side aisles. People came here to work, do business or simply chat with friends.

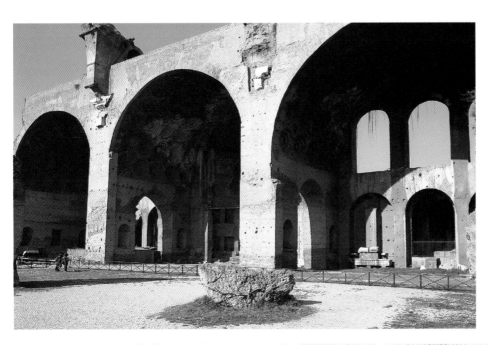

Shopping – Roman Style

IN MOST LARGE TOWNS, shops spread out from the forum and along the main streets. Shops were usually small, family-run businesses. At the start of the working day, shutters or blinds would be taken from the shop front and goods put on display. Noise would soon fill the air as bakers, butchers, fishmongers, fruit and vegetable sellers all began crying out that their produce was the best and cheapest. Joints of meat might be hung from a pole, while ready-cooked food, grains or oils would be sold from pots set into a stone counter. Other shops sold pottery lamps or bronze lanterns, kitchen pots and pans or knives, while some traders repaired shoes or laundered cloth. Hammering and banging coming from the workshops at the back added to the clamour of a busy main street.

ROMAN MONEY
The same currency was used throughout the Roman Empire. Coins were made of gold, silver and bronze. Shoppers kept their money in purses made of cloth or leather or in wooden boxes.

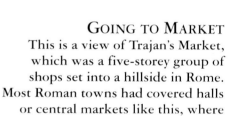

HOW'S BUSINESS?
This carving shows merchants discussing prices and profits while an assistant brings out goods from the stockroom. Most Roman shops were single rooms, with stores or workshops at the back.

GOING TO MARKET
This is a view of Trajan's Market, which was a five-storey group of shops set into a hillside in Rome. Most Roman towns had covered halls or central markets like this, where shops were rented out to traders.

A ROMAN DELICATESSEN

About 1,700 years ago this was the place to buy good food in Ostia, the seaport nearest to Rome. Bars, inns and cafés were fitted with stone counters that were often decorated with coloured marble. At lunchtime, bars like this would be busy with customers enjoying a meal.

A BUTCHER'S SHOP

A Roman butcher uses a cleaver to prepare chops while a customer waits for her order. Butchers' shops have changed very little over the ages – pork, lamb and beef were sold, and sausages were popular, too. On the right hangs a steelyard, a metal bar with a pan like a scale, for weighing the meat.

DISHING IT UP

These are the remains of a shop that sold food. Set into the marble counter are big pottery containers, called *dolia*. These were used for displaying and serving up food, such as beans and lentils. They were also used for keeping jars of wine cool on hot summer days. The containers could be covered with wooden or stone lids to keep out the flies.

Trades and Crafts

THERE WERE POTTERY WORKSHOPS throughout the Roman Empire. Clay pots were made by turning and shaping wet clay on a wheel and baking it in a kiln. Some of the best clay came from the district of Arretium, in Italy. Large pottery centres in Gaul (present-day France) produced a very popular red pottery called Samian ware. In Roman Germany, pottery drinking cups were coloured black and decorated in white with mottoes such as "Drink Up!" or "Bring Me Wine!" – in Latin, of course!

The Romans learned from the Syrians how to blow glass into shapes on the end of a long tube. This was a new and simple technique, although ways of making glass had been known for centuries. As a result, glass became widely used in Roman times.

The skills of the blacksmith were called for everyday, all over the Empire. Smiths hammered away on their anvils, shaping iron tools, weapons and pots. Some metalworkers were fine artists, working in gold, silver and bronze.

THE BLACKSMITHS' GOD
The Romans believed in many different gods. This is a statue of Vulcan, the god of smiths, or metal-workers. He is holding a hammer, used to shape hot metal on an anvil.

COPPERSMITHS
A typical busy day at a coppersmiths' workshop. A customer and his son look on as one of the smiths hammers out sheets of hot copper on an anvil. Another smith is bent over his work, decorating a copper bowl. The goods they are selling are displayed on the wall and hung from the ceiling.

SAMIAN POTTERY

This decorated bowl was found at Felixstowe, in Britain. Glossy red Samian ware was made in Gaul (present-day France), in workshops almost as big as factories. This popular pottery was transported all over the Empire, by land and by sea.

ROMAN SHOP

This stone carving shows a Roman shop with cloth and cushions for sale. Customers are seated while the shopkeeper shows them his wares. The Romans were skilled sculptors and much of our knowledge about the Empire comes from detailed carvings in stone such as this one.

NATURAL DYES

Roman textile workers used a variety of natural dyes on cloth, including onion skins (a golden yellow dye), pine cones (a reddish-yellow dye) and tree bark (a reddish-brown dye). Other natural sources included berries, leaves, minerals, shellfish, nettles and saffron from crocuses.

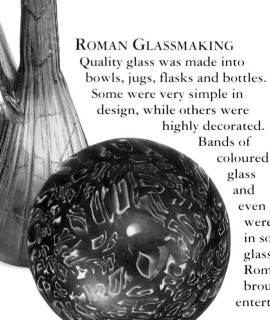

ROMAN GLASSMAKING

Quality glass was made into bowls, jugs, flasks and bottles. Some were very simple in design, while others were highly decorated. Bands of coloured glass and even gold were used in some pieces. The finest glassware was used by wealthy Romans, and was always brought out when they entertained guests.

bark

fir cones

onion

Pictures and Statues

THE ROMANS loved to decorate their homes and public places with paintings and statues. Mosaics were pictures made using *tesserae* – cubes of stone, pottery or glass – which were pressed into soft cement. Mosaic pictures might show hunting scenes, the harvest or Roman gods. Geometric patterns were popular and often used as borders.

Wall paintings, or murals, often showed garden scenes, birds and animals or heroes and goddesses. They were painted on to wooden panels or directly on to the wall. Roman artists loved to trick the eye by painting false columns, archways and shelves. The Romans were skilled sculptors, using stone, marble and bronze. They imitated the ancient Greeks in putting up marble statues in public places and gardens. These might be of gods and goddesses or emperors and generals.

A COUNTRY SCENE
This man and wild boar are part of a mosaic made in Roman North Africa. Making a mosaic was quite tricky – rather like doing a jigsaw puzzle. Even so, skilled artists could create lifelike scenes from cubes of coloured glass, pottery and stone.

SCULPTURE
Statues of metal or stone were often placed in gardens. This bronze figure is in the remains of a house in Pompeii. It is of a faun, a god of the countryside.

FLOOR MOSAICS
Birds, animals, plants and country scenes were popular subjects for mosaics. These parrots are part of a much larger, and quite elaborate, floor mosaic from a Roman house.

MAKE A MOSAIC

You will need: rough paper, pencil, ruler, scissors, large sheet of card, self-drying clay, rolling pin, wooden board, modelling knife, acrylic paints, paintbrush, water pot, clear varnish and brush (optional), plaster paste, spreader, muslin rag.

1 Sketch out your mosaic design on rough paper. A simple design like this one is good to start with. Cut the card so it measures 25cm x 10cm. Copy the design on to it.

2 Roll out the clay on the board. Use the ruler to measure out small squares on the clay. Cut them out with the modelling knife. Leave to dry. These will be your tesserae.

3 Paint the pieces in batches of different colours, as shown above. When the paint is dry, you can coat them with clear varnish for extra strength and shine. Leave to dry.

MOSAIC MATERIALS

Mosaics were often made inside frames, in workshops, and then transported to where they were to be used. Sometimes, the tesserae were brought to the site and fitted on the spot by the workers. The floor of an average room in a Roman town house might need over 100,000 pieces.

tesserae

pot shards

MUSICIANS AND DANCERS

This dramatic painting is on the walls of an excavated villa in Pompeii. It is one in a series of paintings that show the secret rites, or mysteries, honouring the god Dionysus.

REAL OR FAKE?

Roman artists liked to make painted objects appear real enough to touch. This bowl of fruit on a shelf is typical of this style of painting. It was found on the wall of a villa that belonged to a wealthy Roman landowner.

4 Spread the plaster paste on to the card, a small part at a time. While it is still wet, press in your tesserae following the design, as shown. Use your sketch as an extra guide.

5 When the mosaic is dry, use the muslin rag to polish up the surface. Any other soft, dry cloth would also be suitable. Now your mosaic is ready for display.

The Romans liked to have mosaics in their homes. Wealthy people often had elaborate mosaics in their courtyards and dining rooms, as these were rooms that visitors would see.

Doctors and Medicine

SOME ROMANS lived to a ripe old age, but most died before they reached the age of 50. Archaeologists have found out a lot about health and disease in Roman times by examining skeletons that have survived. They can tell, for example, how old a person was when they died and their general state of health during their life. Ancient writings also provide information about Roman medical knowledge.

Roman doctors knew very little science. They healed the sick through a mixture of common sense, trust in the gods and magic. Most cures and treatments had come to Rome from the doctors of ancient Greece. The Greeks and Romans also shared the same god of healing, Aesculapius. There were doctors in most parts of the Empire, as well as midwives, dentists and eye specialists. Surgeons operated on wounds received in battle, on broken bones and even skulls.

The only pain killers were made from poppy juice – an operation must have been a terrible ordeal.

A CHEMIST'S SHOP
This pharmacy, or chemist's shop, is run by a woman. This was quite unusual for Roman times, as women were rarely given positions of responsibility. Roman pharmacists collected herbs and often mixed them for doctors.

GODDESS OF HEALTH
Greeks and Romans honoured the daughter of the god Aesculapius as a goddess of health. She was called Hygieia. The word hygienic, which comes from her name, is still used today to mean free of germs.

MEDICINE BOX
Boxes like this one would have been used by Roman doctors to store various drugs. Many of the treatments used by doctors were herbal, and not always pleasant to take!

MEDICAL INSTRUMENTS
The Romans used a variety of surgical and other instruments. These are made in bronze and include a scalpel, forceps and a spatula for mixing and applying various ointments.

TAKING THE CURE

These are the ruins of a medical clinic in Asia Minor (present-day Turkey). It was built around AD150, in honour of Aesculapius, the god of healing. Clinics like this one were known as therapy buildings. People would come to them seeking cures for all kinds of ailments.

BATHING THE BABY

This stone carving from Rome shows a newborn baby being bathed. The Romans were well aware of the importance of regular bathing in clean water. However, childbirth itself was dangerous for both mother and baby. Despite the dangers, the Romans liked to have large families, and many women died giving birth.

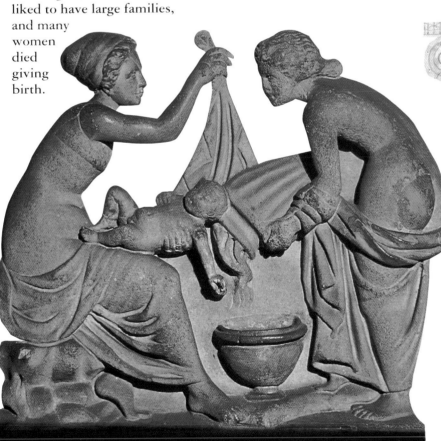

HERBAL MEDICINE

Doctors and travelling healers sold all kinds of potions and ointments. Many were made from herbs such as rosemary, sage and fennel. Other natural remedies included garlic, mustard and cabbage. Many of the remedies would have done little good, but some of them did have the power to heal.

garlic

sage

rosemary

Keeping Clean

tepidarium (warm room)

THE ROMANS may not have all enjoyed good health, but they did like to keep clean. There were public toilets, flushed with constantly flowing water, and people regularly visited public baths. Most towns, even military bases on the frontiers of the Empire, had public bath houses.

The baths were more than just places to wash in. Bathers would meet their friends and spend the afternoon gossiping, in between dips in the bathing pools. Others would exercise, play ball games, or just relax. Businessmen even held meetings at the baths. Men and women used separate rooms or visited the bath house at different times. Slaves would bring bath towels and wooden-soled sandals. Bathers needed the sandals because many of the rooms had hot floors heated by a system of underfloor heating.

OIL FLASK AND STRIGILS
Romans used olive oil instead of soap. They would rub themselves with oil and scrape it off with a curved metal tool called a strigil. The oil would be kept in a small flask, like this one, which has two strigils chained to it.

warm air ducts in walls

BATHING AT BATH
This is a view of the Roman baths in the town of Bath, in Britain. The Romans built the baths there because of the natural hot spring, which bubbled up from the rocks at temperatures of up to 50°C. Rich in health-giving minerals, it attracted visitors from far and wide. This large lead-lined pool was used for swimming. In Roman times, it was covered by a roof.

frigidarium (cold room)

caldarium (hot room)

hot air from furnace

furnace

BATH HOUSE DIG
An archaeological dig in Britain has uncovered these remains of the foundations of a bath house. You can see the bottoms of the pillars that once supported the floor. Hot air from a furnace would have flowed around these pillars, heating the floor and the rooms above it.

THE BATHS
The public baths included exercise areas, changing rooms, a sauna and various pools. The rooms and water were heated by hot air from one or more underground furnaces. The *frigidarium*, or cold room, usually had an unheated pool for bathers to take an icy plunge and was often partly open-air. It led on to a warmer area, the *tepidarium*. In the warmth, bathers would rub themselves with oil, then scrape off any dirt or grime. When they were clean, they were ready to take a dip in the pool. The steamy *caldarium*, or hot room, was nearest to a furnace. Here, bathers could soak or sweat to their hearts' content.

PUBLIC TOILETS
The remains of public toilets like these have been found in many parts of the Empire. People used sponges on sticks to clean themselves. They could rinse the sponges in a channel of flowing water in front of them. Another channel of water, under the stone seats, carried away the waste.

Sport and Combat

MOST ROMANS preferred watching sport rather than taking part themselves. There were some, however, who enjoyed athletics and keeping fit. They took their exercise at the public baths and at the sports ground or *palaestra*. Men would compete at wrestling, long jump and swimming. Women would work out with weights.

Boxing matches and chariot races were always well attended. The races took place on a long, oval racetrack, called a circus. The crowds would watch with such excitement that violent riots often followed. Charioteers and their teams became big stars. Roman crowds also enjoyed watching displays of cruelty. Bloody battles between gladiators and fights among wild animals took place in a special oval arena, called an amphitheatre. Roman entertainments became more spectacular and bloodthirsty as time passed. They would even flood the arenas of amphitheatres for mock sea battles.

A COLOSSEUM
This is the colosseum in the Roman city of El Djem, in Tunisia. A colosseum was a kind of amphitheatre. Arenas such as this were built all over the Empire. The largest and most famous is the Colosseum in Rome.

DEATH OR MERCY?
Gladiators usually fought to the death, but a wounded gladiator could appeal for mercy. The excited crowd would look for the emperor's signal. A thumbs-up meant his life was spared. A thumbs-down meant he must die.

COME ON YOU REDS!

Charioteers belonged to teams and wore their team's colours when they raced. Some also wore protective leather helmets, like the one in this mosaic. In Rome, there were four teams – the Reds, Blues, Whites and Greens. Each team had faithful fans and charioteers were every bit as popular as football stars today.

A DAY AT THE RACES

This terracotta carving records an exciting moment at the races. Chariot racing was a passion for most Romans. Chariots were usually pulled by four horses, though just two or as many as six could be used. Accidents and foul play were common as the chariots thundered round the track.

THE CHAMP

Boxing was a deadly sport. Fighters, like this boxer, wore studded thongs instead of padded boxing gloves. Severe injuries, and even brain damage, were probably quite common.

THE GREEK IDEAL

The Romans admired all things Greek, including their love of athletics. This painted Greek vase dates from about 333BC and shows long-distance runners. However, Roman crowds were not interested in athletic contests in the Greek style, such as the Olympic Games.

Music and Drama

MUSIC AND SONGS were an important part of Roman life. Music was played at banquets, at weddings and funerals, at the theatre, in the home, at fights between gladiators and other public events. The Romans played a variety of musical instruments, including double flutes, pan pipes, lyres, cymbals, rattles and tambourines. These had already been well known in either Egypt or Greece. The Romans also had trumpets and horns, and water-powered organs.

Going to the theatre was a popular Roman pastime. The whole idea of drama came from Greece, so Greek comedies and tragedies were often performed. Roman writers produced plays in a similar style, as well as comic sketches and dances. The stage used the stone front of a building as a backdrop. Rising banks of stone or wooden seats curved around it in a half circle.

MUSIC LESSONS
Girls from wealthy families often had music lessons at home. This wall painting shows a girl being taught to play the cithara, a type of lyre. The Romans adopted this harp-like instrument from the Greeks.

THE ENTERTAINERS
This mosaic from Pompeii shows a group of actors in a scene from a Greek play. Actors were always men, playing the parts of women whenever necessary. The role of actors in a play was shown by the colours of their costume and their masks. The piper in this mosaic is wearing the white mask of a female character.

MAKE A MASK

You will need: self-drying clay, wooden board, rolling pin, large bowl, modelling knife, acrylic paints, paintbrush, water pot, scissors, cord, pencil, green paper or card, gardening wire, some coloured beads.

1 Put the clay on the board. Roll it out into a sheet that is bigger than the bowl you are using. Drape it over the bowl and shape it, as shown above.

2 Trim off the edges and cut out eye holes and a mouth. Roll out the clay you trimmed off and cut out a mouth and nose piece, as shown above. Make a small ball of clay, too.

3 Mould the nose on to the mask. Press the small ball of clay into the chin and put the mouth piece over it, as shown. Make a hole on each side of the mask, for the cord.

MUSICIANS
Some of the musicians in this procession are playing the *cornu*, a large curved horn. It was played at religious festivals and funerals, at public games, and by the Roman army.

ACTORS' MASKS
Roman actors wore masks and wigs to show the type of character they were playing. This detail of a mosaic from Rome shows the kind of elaborate masks they wore.

DRAMA IN THE OPEN AIR
Roman theatres were usually open to the sky. These are the ruins of the larger of the two theatres in Pompeii. It could seat up to 50,000 people. It had no roof, but could be covered by an awning to protect the audience from the hot summer sun.

4 When the clay is dry, paint the mask in bright colours. You can paint it like this one, shown above, or you could make up your own design. Leave the paint to dry.

5 Cut two lengths of cord. Thread them through the holes in the side of the mask, as shown. Secure with a knot. Tie the cord around your head when you wear the mask.

6 Draw, cut out and paint some leaf shapes. Thread them on to a length of wire, as shown. Thread beads between some of the leaves. Wind the wire round the top of the mask.

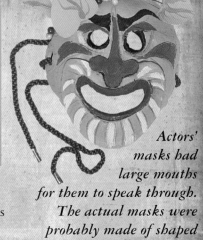

Actors' masks had large mouths for them to speak through. The actual masks were probably made of shaped and stiffened linen.

Fun and Games

Roman children played games such as hide-and-seek, marbles and hopscotch, which are still popular today. Young children played with dolls and little figures of people and animals. These were made of wood, clay or bronze. A child from a wealthy family might be given a child-size chariot, to be pulled along by a goat.

Roman men and women loved playing board games. There were simple games, similar to noughts-and-crosses, and more complicated games, rather like chess or draughts. In some games, players had to race toward the finish. A dice was thrown to decide how many squares they could move at a time. They played with counters made of bone, glass or clay.

The Romans were great gamblers. They would place bets on a chariot race or a cock-fight or on throwing dice. Gambling became such a problem that games of chance were officially banned – except during the winter festival of Saturnalia, when most rules were relaxed. However, the rattle of dice could still be heard in most taverns and public baths.

PLAYING KNUCKLEBONES
Two women play the popular game of knucklebones, or *astragali*. The idea was to throw the knucklebones in the air and catch as many of them as possible on the back of your hand. The number you caught was your score.

MARBLES
Roman children played with these marbles many centuries ago. Two are glass and one is made of pottery. Marbles were either rolled together or on to marked gaming boards. They were also thrown into pottery vases. Nuts, such as hazelnuts and walnuts, were often used like marbles.

KNUCKLEBONES
Most Romans used the ankle bones of sheep to play knucklebones. These had six sides and were also used as dice – each side had a different value. Wealthy Romans might use knucklebones made of glass, bronze or onyx, like these.

MAKE A ROMAN GAME
You will need: self-drying clay, rolling pin, chopping board, modelling knife, ruler, glass tiles for making mosaics, two beads (in the same colours as your tiles).

1 Roll out the clay and trim it to about 25cm square. Use the ruler and knife to mark out a grid, 8 squares across and down, leaving a border around the edge.

2 Decorate the border using the clay you trimmed off, as shown above. Leave to dry. Each player chooses a colour and has 16 tiles and a bead – this is the *dux* or leader.

3 Players take turns to put their tiles on any squares, two at a time. The dux is put on last. Players now take turns to move a tile one square forward, backward or sideways.

JUST ROLLING ALONG

Children from poor families had few toys and had to work from a young age. However, even poor children found time to play, and made do with whatever was at hand. This boy is rolling wheels in front of him as he runs.

YOUR THROW!

This mosaic from Roman North Africa shows three men playing dice games in a tavern. The Romans loved to gamble and would bet on anything, including the roll of the dice. Large amounts could be won or lost on the score when the dice stopped rolling!

COUNTERS

These gaming counters are made of bone and ivory. As well as using quite plain, round ones, the Romans liked to use counters carved in intricate shapes. Here you can see a ram's head, a hare and a lobster. The large round counter has two women carved on it.

DICE

Dice games were played by the poor and the rich. These dice have survived over the centuries. The largest is made of greenstone, the next is made of rock crystal, and the smallest is agate. The silver dice in the form of squatting figures were probably used by wealthy Romans.

During the game, you must move a tile or dux if it is possible to do so – even if it means being captured. The winner is the first player to capture all of the other player's tiles and dux.

4 If you sandwich your opponent's tile between two of yours, it is captured and removed. You then get an extra go. The dux is captured in the same way as any tile.

5 The dux can also jump over a tile to an empty square, as shown. If your opponent's tile is then trapped between your dux and one of your tiles, it is captured.

49

Religions and Festivals

THE ROMANS believed in many different gods and goddesses. Some of them were the same as the gods of ancient Greece, but with different names. Jupiter, the sky god, was the most powerful of all. Venus was the goddess of love, Mars was the god of war, Ceres the god of the harvest, Saturn the god of farmers, and Mercury of merchants. Household gods protected the home. Splendid temples were built in honour of the gods. The Pantheon, in Rome, is the largest and most famous. Special festivals for the gods were held during the year, with processions, music, offerings and animal sacrifices. The festivals were often public holidays. The mid-winter festival of Saturnalia, in honour of Saturn, lasted up to seven days.

As the Empire grew, many Romans adopted the religions of other peoples, such as the Egyptians and the Persians.

JUPITER
Jupiter was the chief god of the Romans. He was the all-powerful god of the sky. The Romans believed he showed his anger by hurling a thunderbolt to the ground.

THE PANTHEON
The Pantheon in Rome was a temple to all the gods. It was built between AD118 and 128. Its mosaic floor, interior columns and high dome still remain exactly as they were built.

DIANA THE HUNTRESS
Diana was the goddess of hunting and the Moon. In this detail from a floor mosaic, she is shown poised with a bow and arrow, ready for the hunt. Roman gods were often the same as the Greek ones, but were given different names. Diana's Greek name was Artemis.

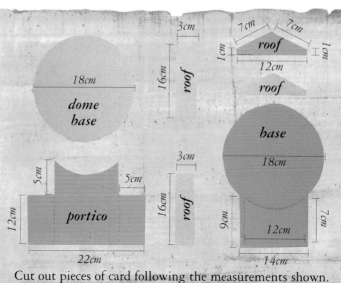

A TEMPLE TO THE GODS

You will need: thick stiff card, thin card, old newspaper, scissors, balloon, PVA glue, ruler, pencils, masking tape, drinking straws, acrylic paints, paintbrush, water pot, Plasticine.

dome base — 18cm

roof — 16cm

3cm

7cm / 7cm
1cm — roof — 1cm
12cm

roof

base — 18cm

portico — 5cm, 5cm, 12cm, 22cm

roof — 16cm, 3cm

9cm, 12cm, 7cm, 14cm

Cut out pieces of card following the measurements shown.

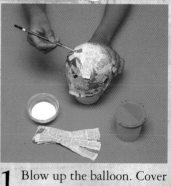

1 Blow up the balloon. Cover it in strips of newspaper pasted on with glue. Keep pasting until you have a thick layer. Leave to dry. Then burst the balloon and cut out a dome.

PRIESTS OF ISIS

The Egyptian mother-goddess Isis had many followers throughout the Roman Empire. This painting shows priests and worshippers of Isis taking part in a water purification ceremony. The ceremony would have been performed every afternoon.

BLESS THIS HOUSE

This is a bronze statue of a *lar* or household god. Originally gods of the countryside, the *lares* were believed to look after the family and the home. Every Roman home had a shrine to the *lares*. The family, including the children, would make daily offerings to the gods.

MITHRAS THE BULL-SLAYER

Mithras was the Persian god of light. He is shown here, in a marble relief from a temple, slaying a bull. This bull's blood was believed to have brought life to the Earth. The cult of Mithras spread through the whole Empire, and was particularly popular with Roman soldiers. However, only men were allowed to worship Mithras.

The Pantheon was built of brick and then clad in stone and marble. Its huge dome, with a diameter of over 43m, was the largest ever constructed until the 1900s.

2 Put the dome on its card base and draw its outline. Cut out the centre of the base to make a halo shape. Make a hole in the top of the dome. Bind the pieces together, as shown.

3 Glue together the base pieces. Cut a piece of thin card long enough to go round the base circle. This will be the circular wall. Use masking tape to hold the portico in shape.

4 Cut some straws into eight pieces, each 6cm long. These will be the columns for the entrance colonnade. Glue together the roof for the entrance. Secure with tape.

5 Glue together the larger pieces, as shown. Position each straw column with a small piece of Plasticine at its base. Glue on the entrance roof. Paint your model.

Family Occasions

THE FAMILY was very important to Romans. The father was the all-powerful head of the family, which included everyone in the household – wife, children, slaves, and even close relatives. In the early days of Rome, a father had the power of life and death over his children! However, Roman fathers were rarely harsh and children were much loved by both parents.

Childhood was fairly short. Parents would arrange for a girl to be betrothed at the age of 12, and a boy at 14. Marriages took place a few years later. Brides usually wore a white dress and a yellow cloak, with an orange veil and a wreath of sweetly-scented flowers. A sacrifice would be made to the gods, and everyone would wish the couple well. That evening, a procession with flaming torches and flute music would lead the newly-weds to their home.

Funerals were also marked with music and processions. By Roman law, burials and cremations had to take place outside the city walls.

HAPPY FAMILIES

This Roman tombstone from Germany shows a family gathered together for a meal. From the Latin inscription on it, we know that it was put up by a soldier of the legions, in memory of his dead wife. He lovingly describes her as the "sweetest and purest" of women.

MOTHER AND BABY

A mother tenderly places her baby in the cradle. When children were born, they were laid at the feet of their father. If he accepted the child into the family, he would pick it up. In wealthy families, a birth was a great joy, but for poorer families it just meant another mouth to feed. Romans named a girl on the 8th day after the birth, and a boy on the 9th day. The child was given a *bulla*, a charm to ward off evil spirits.

TOGETHERNESS

When a couple were engaged, they would exchange gifts as a symbol of their devotion to each other. A ring like this one might have been given by a man to his future bride. The clasped hands symbolize marriage. Gold pendants with similar patterns were also popular.

MOURNING THE DEAD

A wealthy Roman has died and his family have gone into mourning. Laments are played on flutes as they prepare his body for the funeral procession. The Romans believed that the dead went to Hades, the Underworld, which lay beyond the river of the dead. A coin was placed in the corpse's mouth, to pay the ferryman. Food and drink for the journey was buried with the body.

TILL DEATH US DO PART

A Roman marriage ceremony was rather like a present-day Christian wedding. The couple would exchange vows and clasp hands to symbolize their union. Here, the groom is holding the marriage contract, which would have been drawn up before the ceremony. Not everyone found happiness, however, and divorce was quite common.

WEDDING FLOWERS

Roman brides wore a veil on their wedding day. This was often crowned with a wreath of flowers. In the early days of the Empire, verbena and sweet marjoram were a popular combination. Later fashions included orange blossom and myrtle, whose fragrant flowers were sacred to Venus, the goddess of love.

orange blossom

verbena

Soldiers of the Legion

THE ARMY OF THE EARLY EMPIRE was divided into 28 groups called legions. Each of these numbered about 5,500 soldiers. The legion included mounted troops and foot-soldiers. They were organized into cohorts, of about 500 men, and centuries, of about 80 men – even though centuries means 'hundreds'. Each legion was led into battle by soldiers carrying standards. These were decorated poles that represented the honour and bravery of the legion.

The first Roman soldiers were called up from the wealthier families in times of war. These conscripts had to supply their own weapons. In later years, the Roman army became paid professionals, with legionaries recruited from all citizens. During the period of the Empire, many foreign troops also fought for Rome as auxiliary soldiers.

Army life was tough and discipline was severe. After a long march carrying heavy kits, tents, tools and weapons, the weary soldiers would have to dig camp defences. A sentry who deserted his post would be beaten to death.

AT WAR
Trajan's Column in Rome is decorated with scenes from the Dacian wars. These were fought in the region of present-day Romania. Scenes like these can tell us much about Roman soldiers, the weapons they used, their enemies and their allies.

A LEGIONARY
This bronze statue of a legionary is about 1,800 years old. He is wearing a crested parade helmet and the overlapping bronze armour of the period. Legionaries underwent strict training and were brutally disciplined. They were tough soldiers and quite a force to be reckoned with.

ON HORSEBACK
Roman foot-soldiers were backed up by mounted troops, or cavalry. They were divided into groups, of 500 to 1,000, called *alae*. The cavalry were amongst the highest paid of Roman soldiers.

Raising the Standard

The Emperor Constantine addresses his troops, probably congratulating them on a victory. They are carrying standards, emblems of each legion. Standards were decorated with gold eagles, hands, wreaths and banners called *vexilla*. They were symbols of the honour and bravery of the legion and had to be protected at all costs.

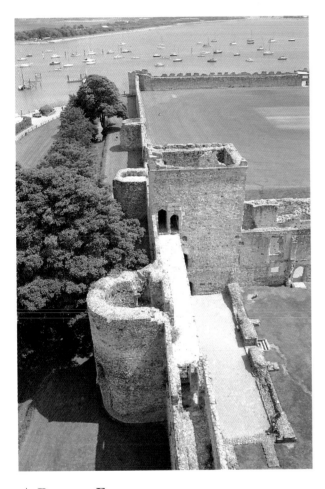

A Roman Fort

The Roman army built forts of wood or stone all over the Empire. This fort is in southern Britain. It was built to defend the coast against attacks by Saxon raiders from northern Europe. Today, its surrounding area is called Porchester. The name comes from a combination of the word port and *caster*, the Latin word for fort.

Hadrian's Wall

This is part of Hadrian's Wall, which marks the most northerly border of the Roman Empire. It stretches for 120km across northern England, almost from coast to coast. It was built as a defensive barrier between AD122 and 128, at the command of the Emperor Hadrian.

Weapons and Armour

ROMAN SOLDIERS were well equipped. A legionary was armed with a dagger, called a *pugio*, and a short iron sword, called a *gladius*, which was used for stabbing and slashing. He carried a javelin, or *pilum*, made of iron and wood. In the early days, a foot-soldier's armour was a mail shirt, worn over a short, thick tunic. Officers wore a cuirass, a bronze casing that protected the chest and back. By about AD35, the mail shirt was being replaced by plate armour made of iron. The metal sections were joined by hooks or by leather straps. Officers wore varying crests to show their rank. Early shields were oval, and later ones were oblong with curved edges. They were made of layers of wood glued together, covered in leather and linen. A metal boss, or cover, over the central handle could be used to hit an enemy who got too close.

HEAD GEAR
Helmets were designed to protect the sides of the head and the neck. This cavalry helmet is made of bronze and iron. It would have been worn by an auxiliary, a foreign soldier fighting for Rome sometime after AD43. Officers wore crests on their helmets, so that their men could see them during battle.

ROMAN SOLDIERS
Artists over the ages have been inspired by the battles of the Roman legions. They imagined how fully armed Roman soldiers might have looked. This picture shows a young officer giving orders.

ROMAN ARMOUR

You will need: tape measure, A1-size sheets of silver card (one or two, depending on how big you are), scissors, pencil, PVA glue, paintbrush, 2m length of cord, compass.

1 Measure yourself around your chest. Cut out three strips of card, 5cm wide and long enough to go round you. Cut out some thinner strips to stick these three together.

2 Lay the wide strips flat and glue them together with the thin strips, as shown above. The Romans would have used leather straps to hold the wide metal pieces together.

3 When the glue is dry, bend the ends together, silver side out. Make a hole in the end of each strip and thread the cord through, as shown above.

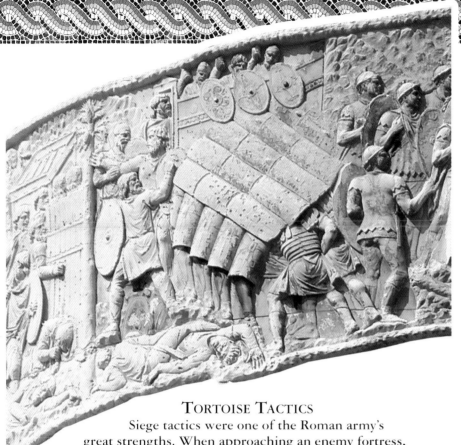

TORTOISE TACTICS

Siege tactics were one of the Roman army's great strengths. When approaching an enemy fortress, a group of soldiers could lock their shields together over their heads and crouch under them. Protected by their shields, they could safely advance toward the enemy. This was known as the tortoise, or *testudo,* formation. During a siege, catapults were used to hurl iron bolts and large stones over fortress walls.

DEADLY WEAPONS

These iron spearheads were found on the site of an old Roman fort near Bath, in Britain. The wooden shafts they were on rotted long ago. Roman soldiers carried both light and heavy spears. The lighter ones were used for throwing, and the heavier ones were for thrusting at close range.

SWORDS

Both short and long swords would have been kept in a scabbard. This spectacular scabbard was owned by an officer who served the Emperor Tiberius. It may have been given to him by the emperor himself. It is elaborately decorated in gold and silver.

Put the shoulder piece over your head and tie the chest section round yourself. Now you are a legionary ready to do battle with the enemies of Rome. Metal strip armour was invented during the reign of the Emperor Tiberius, AD14-37. Originally, the various parts were hinged and were joined together either by hooks or by buckles and straps.

4 Cut a square of card as wide as your shoulders. Use the compass to draw a 12cm diameter circle in the centre. Cut the square in half and cut away the half circles.

5 Use smaller strips of card to glue the shoulder halves together, leaving a neck hole. Cut out four more strips, two a little shorter than the others. Attach them in the same way.

Ships and Sailors

THE ROMANS USED SHIPS for trade, transport and warfare. Roman warships were slim, fast vessels called galleys. They were powered by oarsmen who sat below deck. A standard Roman war galley had 270 oarsmen. It also had a large, square sail that was used for more speed when the wind was favourable.

All kinds of goods, from wool and pottery to marble and grain, had to be moved around the Empire. Most goods, especially heavy cargoes of food or building materials, were moved by water. Merchant ships were deeper, heavier and slower than galleys. They had big, flapping sails and longer oars to make steering easier. Barges were used on rivers.

CONTAINERS
Oil and wine were often shipped in large pottery jars called *amphorae*. Here, an amphora is being carried from one ship to another. The amphorae were usually stacked in the ship's hold, with layers of brushwood as padding.

AT THE DOCKS
This wall painting from the port of Ostia shows a merchant ship being loaded. Heavy sacks of grain are being carried on board. You can see the two large steering oars at the stern, or rear, of the ship.

The Romans built lighthouses on treacherous coasts – stone towers topped by big lanterns or blazing beacons. Pirates, uncharted waters and the weather also made sea travel dangerous.

ROLLING ON THE RIVER
Wine and other liquids were sometimes stored in barrels. These were transported by river barges, like the one in this carving. Barrels of wine would be hauled from the vineyards of Germany or southern France to the nearest seaport.

MAKE AN AMPHORA
You will need: large sheet of thin card, ruler, two pencils, scissors, corrugated cardboard – two circles of 10cm and 20cm in diameter, two strips of 40cm x 30cm and another large piece, masking tape, PVA glue, old newspaper, paintbrush, reddish-brown acrylic paint, water pot.

1 Cut two pieces of card – 5cm and 38cm in depth. Tape the short piece to the small circle. Curl the long piece to make the neck. Make two holes in the side and tape it to the large circle.

2 Roll up the strips of corrugated cardboard. Bend them, as shown, fitting one end to the hole in the neck and the other to the cardboard. Fix in place with glue and tape.

3 Cut a piece of card, 40cm square. Roll it into a cylinder shape. Cut four lines, 10cm long, at one end, so it can be tapered into a point, as shown. Bind with tape.

SAILING OFF TO BATTLE

This painting imagines the impressive spectacle of a Roman war galley leaving harbour on its way to battle. Galleys were powered by rows of oarsmen, who sat on benches below deck. The helmsman, who controlled the galley's steering, shouted orders down to them. This galley has three banks, or layers, of oars. An underwater battering ram stuck out from the bow, or front, of war galleys. During a sea battle, the mast was lowered and the galley would try to ram the enemy ship. With the ram stuck in its side, Roman soldiers could easily board the enemy ship to finish the fight man to man.

An amphora like this one might have been used to carry wine, oil or fish sauce. Its long, pointed end would be stuck into layers of brushwood for support during transport.

4 To give the amphora a more solid base, roll up a cone of corrugated cardboard and stick it around the tapered end. Push a pencil into the end, as shown. Tape in position.

5 Stick the neck on to the main body. Cover the whole piece with strips of newspaper brushed on with glue. Leave to dry. Repeat until you have built up a thick layer.

6 When the paper is dry, paint the amphora. Roman amphorae were made of clay, so use a reddish-brown paint to make yours look like it is clay. Leave to dry.

59

Builders of the Empire

THE ROMANS were great builders and engineers. As the legions conquered foreign lands, they built new roads to carry their supplies and messengers. The roads were very straight, stretching across hundreds of kilometres. They were built with a slight hump in the middle so that rainwater drained off to the sides. Some were paved with stone and others were covered with gravel or stone chippings. Roman engineers also used their skills to bring water supplies to their cities by building aqueducts.

The Romans constructed great domes, arched bridges and grand public buildings all across the Empire. Local supplies of stone and timber were used. Stone was an important Roman building material, but had to be quarried and transported to sites. The Romans were the first to develop concrete, which was cheaper and stronger than stone.

The rule of the Romans came to an end in western Europe over 1,500 years ago. Yet reminders of their skills and organization are still visible today.

ROMAN ROADS
A typical Roman road, stretching into the distance as far as the eye can see. It runs through the coastal town of Ostia, in Italy. It was the 1800s before anyone in Europe could build roads to match those of ancient Rome.

MUSCLE POWER
This stone carving shows how Romans used big wooden cranes to lift heavy building materials. The crane is powered by a huge treadwheel. Slaves walk round and round in the wheel, making it turn. The turning wheel pulls on the rope, that is tied round the heavy block of stone, raising it off the ground.

MAKE A GROMA

You will need: large, strong piece of cardboard, scissors, ruler, pencil, square of card, PVA glue, masking tape, balsa wood pole, Plasticine, silver foil, string, large sewing needle, acrylic paints, paintbrush, water pot, broom handle.

1 Cut out three pieces of cardboard – two 20cm x 6cm, one 40cm x 6cm. Cut another piece, 15cm x 12cm, for the handle. Then cut them into shape, as shown above.

2 Measure to the centre of the long piece. Use a pencil to make a slot here, between the layers of cardboard. The slot is for the balsa wood pole.

3 Slide the balsa wood pole into the slot and tape the cardboard pieces in a cross. Use the card square to make sure the four arms of the groma are at right angles. Glue in place.

BUILDING MATERIALS

The Romans used a variety of stones for building. Local quarries were the most common source. Limestone and a volcanic rock called tufa were used in Pompeii. Slate was used for roofing in parts of Britain. Fine marble, used for temples and other public buildings, was available in the Carrara region of Italy, as it still is today. However, it was also imported from overseas.

marble

slate

SURVIVING THE CENTURIES

This Roman bridge crosses the River Guadalquivir at Cordoba in Spain. The Romans had no bulldozers or power tools, and yet their buildings and monuments have survived thousands of years.

WALLS OF ROME

The city of Rome's defences were built at many stages in its history. These sturdy walls were raised during the reign of the Emperor Marcus Aurelius, AD121–180. Known as the Aurelian Walls, they are still in good condition today.

Slot the arms on to the balsa wood pole. Use the plumb lines as a guide to make sure the pole is vertical. The arms can then be used to line up objects in the distance. Romans used a groma to measure right angles and to make sure roads were straight.

4 Roll the Plasticine into four small cones and cover them with foil. Thread string through the tops, as shown. These are the groma's plumb lines, or vertical guides.

5 Tie the plumb lines to each arm, as shown. They must all hang at the same length – 20cm will do. If the Plasticine is too heavy, use wet newspaper rolled up in the foil.

6 Split the top of the handle piece, and wrap it round the balsa wood pole. Glue it in place, as shown. Do the same on the other end with the broom handle. Paint the groma.

Glossary

A

amphitheatre An oval open-air arena surrounded by seats. It was invented by the Romans for public shows, such as gladiators fighting to the death and battles between wild animals.

amphora (plural: amphorae) A pottery storage jar, often shaped like a tall vase with handles and a pointed base. Amphorae came in all shapes and sizes – tall and slim, fat and round.

anvil A block used by smiths for shaping hot metals.

aqueduct

aqueduct An artificial channel for carrying water over a long distance. Aqueducts were usually underground or were supported on arched bridges.

arena The sand floor area in an amphitheatre where games and combats took place.

atrium The hallway or courtyard in a Roman house. The centre of the atrium was open to the sky.

auxiliaries Soldiers recruited from non-Roman citizens.

B

basilica A huge building in the forum of a Roman city. It was a cross between a town hall and law courts.

blacksmith A craftsman who makes or repairs iron goods.

brazier A bronze container filled with hot coals, used for heating rooms.

C

catapult A large wooden structure used during a siege to fire stones and iron bolts at the enemy.

chariot

century A unit of the Roman army, numbering from 80 to 100 soldiers.

chariot A lightweight cart drawn by horses. Chariots were used in warfare or for racing.

circus An oval track used for chariot races.

citizen A free person with the right to vote.

civilization A society that has made advances in the arts, science and technology, law or government.

cohort A division of the Roman army, at times numbering about 500 soldiers.

conscript Someone who is called up by the government to serve in the army.

consul One of the two leaders of the Roman republic, elected each year.

cremation The burning of dead bodies.

Consul

cuirass Armour that protects the upper part of the body.

curia The council in ancient Roman cities.

D

dictator A ruler with total power.

E

emperor The ruler of an empire.

empire A large number of different lands ruled over by a single person or government.

estate A large amount of land, houses and farms, usually owned by a single person or group.

F

flax A plant whose stems are used to make a cloth called linen. Its blue flowers can be used to make a dye, and its seeds are crushed to produce linseed oil.

forceps Surgical instruments shaped like pincers or tongs.

forum The town centre or downtown area of a Roman city.

G

galley A warship powered by oars.

gladiator A professional fighter, a slave or a criminal who fought to the death for public entertainment.

graffiti Words or pictures scrawled or scratched in public places, particularly on walls.

grid pattern A criss-cross pattern of straight lines at right angles. It was used to divide a town into blocks and straight streets.

groma An instrument used by Roman surveyors. They used it to measure right angles and to make sure roads were straight.

gruel A soup of cereal and water, such as porridge.

guild A society which protected the interests of people working within a trade.

J

javelin A throwing spear.

K

kiln An industrial oven, or a furnace.

kindling Twigs, woodchips or other material used to start a fire.

L

legion A section of the Roman army made up only

legionary

of Roman citizens. Non-Roman citizens could not be legionaries.

litter A form of transport in which a seat or platform is carried by bearers.

lyre One of various harp-like instruments played in ancient Greece and Rome.

M

mail Chain armour, made up of interlocking iron rings.

midwife Someone who helps a woman to give birth.

mosaic

mosaic A picture made up from many small squares or cubes of glass, stone or pottery, set in soft concrete.

myrrh A kind of resin from shrubs, used to make perfume and medicine.

O

ochre A kind of yellow or reddish-coloured earth.

P

palla A veil worn over the head or shoulders by Roman women.

panpipes A musical instrument, made up of a series of pipes of different lengths.

papyrus A tall reed that grows in the River Nile, used to make a kind of paper.

patrician A member of one of the old, wealthy and powerful families in ancient Rome.

plate armour Fitted body armour made of linked sheets of solid metal.

plebeian A member of the (free) common people of ancient Rome.

preserve To treat food so that it does not spoil or go bad.

R

ram A large, pointed beam extending from the hull, or front, of an ancient warship. It was used to ram into the side of an enemy ship, making it easier to board.

republic A state that is governed by an assembly of its citizens rather than by a king.

S

sacrifice The killing of a living thing in honour of the gods.

Samian ware A type of glazed, red-clay pottery that was popular throughout the Roman Empire.

Samian pot

Saturnalia A winter festival held in honour of the god Saturn.

Senate The law-making assembly of ancient Rome.

sickle A tool with a curved blade used to cut grass or grain crops.

society All the classes of people living in a particular community or country.

standard A banner used by armies to rally their troops in battle or carried in parades.

stola A long dress worn by Roman women. It was worn over a tunic.

oil flask and strigils

strigil A metal scraper used for cleaning the body.

stylus A pointed tool, such as the one used to scratch words on to a wax tablet.

survey To map out and measure land. Land is surveyed before the construction of a building or a road, or any other structure.

T

tablinium The formal reception room and study in a Roman house.

terracotta Baked, unglazed, orange-red clay.

toga A white woollen robe, worn by the upper classes in ancient Rome.

tortoise or testudo A method of covering a group of soldiers with shields to protect them from missiles.

treadwheel A wooden wheel turned by the feet of people, used to power mills or other machinery.

tribune One of the officials elected to represent the interests of the common people in ancient Rome. Tribune was also a rank in the Roman army.

triclinium Dining room. Its name comes from the Roman tradition of having an arrangement of three (tri) couches to lie on while dining.

trident

trident A three-pronged spear used by fishermen and gladiators.

trivet A metal stand placed over a flame to support a cooking pot.

tunic A simple, shirt-like garment.

tutor A personal teacher.

V

villa A Roman country house, often decorated with mosaics and wall paintings. Villas were usually part of an agricultural estate.

Index